A Magnificent
Expression

A MAGNIFICENT EXPRESSION

REV. BROADWAY SWIM

Order this book online at www.trafford.com
or email orders@trafford.com

Most Trafford titles are also available at major online book retailers.

Printed in the United States of America.

ISBN: 978-1-4669-4455-8 (sc)
ISBN: 978-1-4669-4454-1 (e)

Trafford rev. 07/25/2012

 www.trafford.com

North America & international
toll-free: 1 888 232 4444 (USA & Canada)
phone: 250 383 6864 ♦ fax: 812 355 4082

PREFACE

The national News media and their commentators have called for an open conversation on race relations, and since a conversation is the expression of sentiments, observations, opinions and ideas, I am willing to participate. But that conversation should be centered in facts that can define the origin and genuine attributes of the races with documented accounts of what those facts are.

For the past twenty five years I have been searching through historical data for information that could offer some proof that could bring those facts into play. And I found, what I consider to be, a fallacious editing of historical data that can only be interpreted as a breach of honesty. It is the kind of editing that rearranged and deleted factual and definitive aspects of the Black heritage in order to portray the Black man as a deficient being which subjected him to attitudinal attacks on his character.

The author of such editing makes the attempt to portray the Black man as a subspecies individual who draws his survival from the White man. But the moment he makes that attempt he is challenged and defied by his own deficiencies. A deficiency that was overcome by drawings from the creative abilities of the Black man. It seems that the idea of defaming the Black man's character came from his perception of himself.

From those discoveries I drew the conclusion that the American Blacks are as much an heir of American heritage as the Whites, and that we carries with us the potentialities of being the greatest people on earth.

I am not talking about being great through oppressing others. There is no greatness in oppression, only conflict and confusion, which generate fear. And it is the collision of fears that drives men to their graves. And there are too many avoidable graves in America already. Our grave yards are beginning to define our character.

It takes a conversation of revolutionary perceptions with facts and ideas wherewith we can find a compensatory asset of each other that will make racialism a useless observation.

In this expression I am presenting the facts as I underscored them, that you may use their truths to review your observation of the matter.

BY: BROADWAY SWIM

CHAPTER 1

The Birth of A Legacy

The expression of the Black people made its first impression in history through the genius of a Black man whose Biblical name is Nimrod; who, by his intellectual clairvoyance, brought into existence a socio-political sovereignty that shaped the social order of the world, and launched a governing system from which the nations of the world were proliferated. The Bible depicts Nimrod as having an imperial personality, and that he was the first potentate (ruler) on earth (Genesis 10:8 American Standard Bible). His initiative as the first ruler on earth established a kingdom from which the industrial and economical power of the world was first anchored.

The beginning of Nimrod's Kingdom was the city of Babel (The Hebrew term for Babylon), in which he began to build a tower to Heaven (The Tower of Babel). From there he built the cities of Erech, Accad, and Calneh in the land of Shinar. He is termed as a mighty hunter by the Holy Bible, which is fundamental of his ability to provide substance for his people's survival.

Nimrod was the elder son of Cush, who was the eldest grandson of Noah, Ham's first born. (The word, Cush, in the ancient Hebrew language is the designation for 'Black Man'. Ethiopia is the Greek designation for Black Man). During those primeval times, people were named according to their most distinguished characteristic or preconceived purpose.

The Bible's indication that Nimrod was the begotten son of Cush means that Nimrod was exactly like his father, a Black man.

The opinion of early historians of the White persuasion led the world to believe that Nimrod's status as a mighty hunter meant that he was a vicious apostate. On the contrary, the Biblical ascription of mighty hunter simply imputes Nimrod as being a resourceful King, esteeming him for his ability to regiment, organize, and educate his people in thought, activity, and methods that was instrumental in their survival, and the building of the first Kingdoms on earth. By that, it could be said that he was also the first educationist on earth. The tower he attempt to build in Babel was an architectural phenomenon: a structure which required the thinking of an intellectual genius whose knowledge had to be imparted to his builders, which required instructional seminars to verse them in the arts of architecture.

It is suggested that Nimrod defied God in building the tower of Babel, but in essence Nimrod was thinking like his grandfather, Noah. It is obvious that his decision to build the tower was predicated on the notion that he could save his people from a flood should it occur again. Nimrod's only infraction, as I see it, was his inclination to outguess God.

It is assumed that, since Cush was a Black man his father, Ham was Black. On the contrary, Ham was not a black man. The Name Ham arises out of the Hebrew word, Sheham, which mean brownish or suntan. Therefore, some historians suggested that Cush's color was the result of Noah's curse. But that is not true. The scripture clearly refutes that. The curse was imposed upon Canaan, Ham's youngest son. There were two other brothers and many sisters between Cush and Canaan, possibly accounting for a hundred years or more. And Noah's curse had nothing to do with skin color, or any other member of Ham's family. It was a wrath pertaining only to Canaan's moral nature.

How, then, that Cush was Black? To answer that question I will have to refer you to the ancestry of Ham's wife and implicate her with the six chapter of Genesis where the sons of God came down and married the daughters of men; and to the book of Enoch, chapter eighteen of the apocrypha scripture. In Genesis, the phrase, 'Son of God' was used to define Angels who came down on earth and transformed themselves into the image of men. In the book of Enoch, according to his assessment of his experience when he was taken up into Heaven, they are described as being giants, dark in complexion with the appearance of warriors. Enoch explains how they forsook their abode in Heaven and came down to earth and married the daughters of men.

According to the book of Genesis, the off spring of these Angels were giants, mighty men of old, which mean superior in strength and intelligence.

Now, being that giants were found only in the lineage of Ham, who was light brown-skinned and of normal stature, suggests that Ham's wife carried the genes of those giants, passing their genetic code through the linage of Ham. For, only in the linage of Ham does history show that giants and people of dark color existed. During the days of Abraham those giants were called Zam-zum'mins (Duet. 2: 20, and Rephaims (Genesis 14: 5). History doesn't describe Ham's wife by name, nor reflect on her ancestry, but the circumstances of antediluvian history qualifies the relationship of the antediluvian giants with the primal Cushites which attest to her as being the mother of the Black race of people.

Each family of the sons of Noah established kingdoms. But the first kingdom on earth was established by Nimrod, the son of Cush, which became an empire having many intra-kingdoms of great extent under his sovereign authority.

So supreme was the Excellency of his rule that he was reputed to the stature of a demigod after his death. They worshiped his spirit as the sun god. (Supposedly Marduk). His sister-wife was worshiped as the Queen of Heaven, Astarte, after her death. Reference to her is found in the Book of Jeremiah. Jer. 7:19; 44:17,18,19,25. The epithet "of Heaven" alludes to her astral character, which implied that she was above the tangible world in refinement. Nevertheless, her worship was chiefly the narrative of women. There may be some reference to her in the book of Hosea, Hosea 3:1.

The death of Nimrod did not abort the brilliancy of those Black people. Their ability to lead the world was manifested in all of their doings. Hammurabi, the sixth king of the first Dynasty of Babylon, a descending grandson of Nimrod, further repudiated the genius of the Black people. He continued to form a powerful people, proliferating agriculture, industry, and commerce. Though, religion was establish before his time, he enforced the worship of the sun god, Murduk, who was the chimerical spirit of Nimrod, his predecessor who was thought to had risen to the sun because of his effort to reach the sun by the tower he attempted to build in the city if Babel.

In theory, Hammurabi was an agent of Marduk, profoundly dedicated to the well-being of his people.

Hammurabi created cruciform, which are characters in handwriting. It could be said that he invented writing. He was famous, mostly, for his code of law. He enacted laws governing businesses, and he wrote the first laws governing marriage and divorce.

Normally, a man had only one wife, but if she became permanently sick that she couldn't perform her duties as a wife, he could remarry, provided that he kept his first wife in the house with him and continued to support her. Hammurabi did not advocate divorce.

The laws of Hammurabi began a sense of justice in which today's laws are anchored. Some of the laws of the Old Testament Jews are similar to those enacted by Hammurabi. The epic of the creation was written during his rule.

Black people of those times were distinctively instrumental in creating a commercial system that catered to the survival of the world. Their inventive and marketing skills were the vehicles that powered the whole Eastern economy.

Raamah, a nephew of Nimrod and fourth named son of Cush was the founder of a tribe that was highly renowned as economical marketers (traders). Traders of those times were the heartbeat of world survival. He and his two sons, Sheba and Dedan who were related to Abraham through one of Abraham's mistress, Keturah (First Chronicles 1: 32), created a commercial empire that provided merchandise throughout that region. Their activities are implicated in the Biblical account of world trade during those times (Ezekiel 27: 15 and 22, 23, 24).

The Bible further accounts for the masterfulness of the Black people as a whole (Isaiah 18:1,2 in all Version of the Holy Bible except the King James version). The King James Version was translated in 1611; it was so controversial that it remained off the market for 200 years. The controversy was based on the choice of words the translators used. For example, they used terrible for mighty and suffer for perseverance. And, the way their sentences were structured made it hard to understand the message the original scripture was meant to convey.

I am not suggesting that any one should disregard the King James Version of the Bible, on the contrary, I am suggesting, though, that users of the King James version of the Bible should use other Bibles to help them understand the message intended by the Holy Scripture. Especially if they want the truth about the Black race.

In, or about, the year 950 BC, the queen of Sheba, a Black woman who was the off spring of both Cush and Abraham—see diagram in back of book—known in the Bible as queen of the South (Matt 12: 42) traveled over a 1200 mile trek of desert to visit the rich and powerful King of Israel. History states that she took the journey to convince herself of the truth of the report which had reached her about the Wisdom of Solomon. But, it is certain that her reason were more manifold than that. Her main reason was dictated by commercial interests, to arrange trade treaties with Israel and its allies.

Nevertheless, according to inscription found in southwestern Arabia written in Sebaean characters, she mothered a son for Solomon.

That son gave rise to a nation of Black Jews in Africa that lasted to this day. After more than 2000 years of silence, history has finally affirmed the existence of those Jews. During the Christian era they were called Aksumite Christians who were known as the Zagwe Dynasty.

In 1229 AD, the Zagwes were overthrown by the Amharic royal house from the Ethiopian Kingdom of Shewa who reinstituted the Solomon Dynasty based on their claim of imperial power inherited from King Solomon's son by the queen of Sheba. His name was Menelik the 1st. This conquest gave to the world the implication of imperial mythology of Ethiopia as the New Holy Land, and an impression of the Shewan emperors as the successors of the true African linage of King David of Israel.

History records that after Solomon learned of his son's birth; he made a replica of the Ark and sent it to Africa along with priests to minister to his son. This accounts for the claim that the Ark of the Covenant is in Africa.

But many Black Jews have left Africa, some to America and others to other countries of the world. Most accountable, though, are those who were airlifted to Israel, beginning in the late twentieth century. 35,000 of them had been relocated in Israel by 1990. The relocation is continuing.

CHAPTER 2

The stumbling of a legacy

To make any sense in this next chapter, I would have to go back to the 6 century after Christ:

> Though, the Queen of Sheba was the first ruling queen of an Ethiopian sovereignty, the imperialistic tug of her rule led to Queen-ruled sovereignties in the whole of Africa. Long after her; beginning in 150 BC there were seven dynasties of queens to about 150 AD, all directed their authority toward sensuous intelligence rather than military might, changing the dynamics of Africa's military heritage. The titles of those queens, according to Biblical scripture was Candace or Kandake (Acts 8: 26,27)

Because Biblical scripture, in part, was translated from Hebrew to Greek, and written in Greek and Aramaic during the Christian area, I must stop here to remind readers that the word Ethiopia was translated from the word Cush, and is used progressively in Biblical scripture to describe all Black people when the distinction of races was written in

Greek, except for the one-time use of the word Niger (Acts 13: 1), which was the Aramaic term for Black man.

In the 6th century AD (Some historian put it in the 4th century); the Mohammedans conquered the South West dominion of Ethiopia which then encompassed the Red Sea.

Ethiopians scattered throughout the continent of Africa, establishing tribes that were named according to their chiefs. For centuries they were compelled to pay tribute to the Mohammedans whose dominating influence slowly began to affected their, once, indomitable alliance, individualizing them toward the Mohammedans customs

Many began to speak the Muslim language and adapted the Muslim ethics.

Living under these conditions caused a psychological spin on their nature and they began to exert their frustration toward each other. Though, each tribe was a political part of the whole African statehood, the problems they faced were more embedded in their distrust of each other than in the weight of the Mohammedans' oppression.

It was a swaggering experience. Arrogant and conceitedly, they turned their wrath on each other in Brutal and violent forms, destroying homes and farms of people who were once their neighbors, whose villages were just a stone throw away and their farms had common boundaries, taking spoils and ravishing women who were once treated like sisters. Those who weren't put to the sword were taken prisoner and held in bondage to prevent them from rejoining their warring comrades. All because they had forsaken the ingenious heir-ship of their heritage.

Some of the tribes remained passive though, and established territorial boundaries in the mountain regions until they revived their strength (which eventually became perceptual of statehood), while others settled into the deep reaches of the African jungle, resorting to primitive methods to survive. In all cases the male was chief of a Tribe, except for one tribe in West Africa where a female was the chief figure. This one tribe's culture was so unique that neighboring tribes shunned them as if they were a cursed people. The women treated their husband like indentured servants. At all times they had their way, and when they felt no further use for their husbands, they were free to marry another. But the deserted husband could not engage in any kind of intimate relationship with another woman. The result of which would be severe punishment or death. Because of their chauvinistic custom against the male image, the linage of that tribe was traced back through the mothers to establish a royal heritage to the queens who once ruled in Africa. Thus, setting all Black mothers as the vestige of the Black linage, which is uncommon to the rest of the world.

Why haven't the Black people recovered from such separatist behavioral patterns? Well, no credible evidence based on hard and clear facts is ever given, yet, many historians attempted to explain. But the moment they make that attempt, they are confronted by their own inexpiable convictions. Conviction that is subjective of their own hypothetical ideology. The way they try to explain the African legacy is distorted by supposition and parallelism, based on prejudice and wishy-washy ideas.

Nevertheless, any attempt to explain the schismatic breach in the internal relationship of those Black people is to consider the iconological factors that bore upon the experiences of their imperial nature. Their military superiority had eroded under 300 years of artistic and aesthetic idolatry, and when Christianity was introduced to them in the first century, the passiveness of the Christian philosophy further softened their aggressive nature, and made them more vulnerable to the Muslim's methods to control them (which was repeated by Willie Lynch in the Willie Lynch papers during the American slave era). They were brainwashed to become enemies of themselves. The strong was pitted against the wealthy for recognition; the male was pitted against the female; the young against the old; the poor and the disadvantage were pitted against those who strove successfully, and there was some who were persuaded to believe that their chance for success was being compromised by traitorous neighbors. Then, there were those who strove for success despite the propaganda, and when they got it, employed the benefits of it in the style of the oppressor. They followed the methods of the Mohammedans to hold on to what little privilege they had. The stratagems they used and the confusion they caused turned into a sectarian war that lasted long after the Mohammedans' influence had ebbed. The Mohammedans, who had infiltrated Africa to suppress the onslaught of Christianity, were unable to totally excel the African autonomy because of tribal conflicts ceased to demand their salutation.

Over the years, the lifestyle of some of those tribes became influenced by necromantic rituals—a fanciful medium of assumptions that, when practiced, is believed to conjure the spirit of the dead for purposes of magically revealing the future or influencing the course of events.

The mode and manner of their rituals was later defined as witchcraft and became the stigma of their lifestyle.

Christianity had entered Africa during the apostolic era, before the 1st century AD. It was introduced to the Candace of Ethiopia by her treasurer who is referred too in Biblical scripture as the eunuch of the queen of the Ethiopians (Acts 8: 27). It survived the Muslim influence during the Mohammedans rule because it was the tenet of that tribe isolated from the rest of the African world behind a vast mountain range through the seventh century. The tribe indigenous to that region was the Agews. They had become so detached from the rest of Africa that they totally abandoned their native tongue and their native religion for Aksumite Christianity.

By the 14th century AD, Ethiopia had completely regained its military power, and engaged in an incessant struggle to prevent another Muslim invasion, and to protect the Christian Church in Egypt.

In the 14 century, Amda Tseyon, the fourth Emperor of the Solomonid Dynasty, warned the governors of Egypt that he would divert the waters of the Nile to reduce Egypt to a desert if they didn't desist from persecuting the Copts Christian Church.

Late in the 15th century, when gold became the most convenience means of mercantile exchange, Africa became the focus point of the world's economists because of it large gold reserve.

CHAPTER 3

A Legacy In Jeopardy

In 1483, Henry the Navigator went to Africa to buy gold. It was during the shading and nuance of the renaissance when the whole Eastern world was experiencing a humanistic revival of classical influence.

The warlords of Africa felt the pinch of that influence, but they had accumulated so many prisoners that they lived in apprehension of a mutinous takeover of their tribe by those prisoners, and they were seeking ways to exhaust their prisoner population without compromising their own safety.

Henry's initial effort to by gold was refused, but a compromise was made when he agreed to buy some of the tribe's prisoners. "You buy my prisoners and I'll sell you some gold", was the tribe's strategy. It was a solution to the growing prisoner problem, an irony that put the whole Black race in jeopardy.

Henry the Navigator bought four prisoners from that particular tribe and gave them to the pope, who the pope used as indentured servants. Indentured servitude was a condition befitting slavery, except that it allowed its laborers to go free after six or seven years. This form of servitude was prevalence throughout the Eastern world.

The pope became so impressed with the convenience of having those four prisoners that he required more, and when the news reached abroad, the demands for indentured servants became a profitable market. Thus, the servitude of those African prisoners became so economically feasible that they became a commodity of an engineered science called the 'Slave Trade' that spread throughout the western world. Years later, the mean of securing that commodity changed. What was once an auction caucus became a predatory incursion. When the tribes' prisoner population was exhausted, the traders resorted to kid-napping. In some cases, Native Africans assisted traders in their kid-napping sprees.

But when gold was discovered in North America after the Columbus era, three of the major countries of the world turned their attention west. Spain was the first to fix its flag in the New World. Spanish colonies were established in such places as Mexico, Florida, and California for the purpose of mining silver and gold.

France succeeded Spain to America. Most of the French settled in Canada, the Ohio Valley, and the Louisiana area.

English colonies were founded later. These colonies were located along the Atlantic coast. The first English colony to be established was named Jamestown in the colony state of Virginia. Though, the English settlers considered the Indians they found there as savages, some of them had an uncultivated history themselves. Most of them were criminals who were taken out of jails in England and sent there under the indenture servitude stature to help build the colonies. African, Germans, Portuguese, etc, were in the mix, and their offenses ranged from the failure to pay their debts to felony assaults. But seven years of servitude earned them their freedom, and they became citizens of the colonies.

Most of the settlers made little effort to understand the Indians and their way of life. The Indians were a free people living contingently off nature. They needed no written laws to control their behavior, and they valued honest and courage more than wealth. The intermixing that did occur was mostly for food and material for clothes. And that was negotiated by one of the colonist named John Smith who had befriended a tribal chief and his family through a young girl name Pocahontas, for she had fallen in love with Smith. But a drought stricken the area, the food supply became scarce, and the Indians stopped trading with the colonists to preserve provision for themselves.

The colonists lack of agriculture skills put them at a grave disadvantage. Only a few of them were farmers, not enough to satisfy their demands. Their food supply became so low that they resorted to stealing from the Indians. The Indians took offense of it and retaliated. During the conflict, John Smith was wounded and was sent back to England to recover.

In 1619, on his return to the colonies, his ship encountered a slave ship off the Atlanta coast on its way to Mexico with captives from Africa. He seized the ship and brought it to Jamestown Virginia.

At first thought, the colonists didn't want the captives there. The idea of having slaves made them look back into the far reaches of their own past. It was a reminder of the pathos and sentiments they had experience, couched in terms of the abject lifestyle they had had to endure. It was a terrible disenfranchisement of human dignity that they wished on no man, but the circumstances they faced outweighed their compassion. Their need for farm labors and contingents to help build their intra-structure merited their compromise. The realization of their benefits was clear; they knew the Africans to be industrious people, manually skillful, and creatively inclined. And their war-like disposition was a match for the unruly Indians. And, too, in seven years they would be free to enjoy the fruits of their labor.

The question about the captive's civility was no different from theirs. The seven years they had spent in servitude, in terms of their eventual freedom, helped them to develop the customs and amenities of a civil community, and they assumed the captives would be the same.

The African captives succumb to their appeal with little resistance, mostly because they felt that they would eventually be free to go back to Africa.

In 1621 Anthony Johnson, a black entrepreneur from England, versed in commercial assessments, settled in the colonies. He was to be the catalyst for settling the stagnant economy. The settlers welcomed him, but later disagreed with his radical views toward slavery. He had brought indenture servants from England with him, but he refused to release them from their indentured contract. Some of the settlers, after learning of his dissent, covertly ridiculed him and informed his servants of his violation.

John Caster, one of Johnson's servants who had been with him for more than seven years ran off, using the indenture servitude stature to justify his freedom. When Johnson learned of his estrangement he petitioned the court to recover him, claiming that his servants was chattel property, and that he own them for life. The court ruled in his favor, a decree that turned Indentured servitude into an unrelenting and atrocious form of slavery that lasted for 200 years.

Was Anthony Johnson a traitor? Can we describe his character as a intra-racial bigot—a hater of his own kind? With what better term than a tyrant can we describe a man who deny the people of his own race the chance to be free? To answer that question satisfactorily, we must consider how the circumstances of those days could have develop to effect the world we live in today. First we must realize that the indentured servitude stature would have eventually released thousands, if not millions, of freed slaves into the struggling economical environment of this country. And we must consider the demands those freed slaves would have imposed upon the resources of that environment, and whether that environment had the factors that could possibly contribute to their survival. With every freed slave, their needs, would have added innumerable difficulties to the already existing struggle to survive. And like always, struggling people resorts to struggling means, which oftentimes result in civil conflicts. And the victors of a civil conflict usually become the governing factor of that environment.

Secondly, it could be considered that as the slave market flooded the country with slaves over the years the number of freed slaves would eventually outnumber the central population. And to transform them from their African peculiarities to homogenize them into the culture of the new world without some kind of oppressive leverage was hardly an achievable task.

Considering these political aspects, despite the cruel and satanic nature that slavery turned out to be, Anthony Johnson could very well be described as a patriot. For, without his victory in court, the possibility of this country becoming an Africanized nation was very likely.

CHAPTER 4

Oppressive persuasion

History is a funny thing. No sooner than it had mentioned how collectively disenfranchised the slaves were under the oppression of their masters did it show some signs of hope for redemption. Though, the hope were guised in a psychologically persuasive method called Meritorious Manumission, it had no real affect on the freedom of the slave as a hold. It was aimed at that class of slaves who were so partial to the American way of life, which had denied their freedom, that they could not help but react to the incentives and rewards that Meritorious Manumission offered them. An incentive that was aimed at neutralizing the slaves allegiance to each other, and destined to result in betrayal and distrust.

Meritorious Manumission was a stature that allowed a slave to go free based on his merit, which was determined by their unquestionable commitment to the benefit of their master, such as saving a taskmaster's life, inventing something useful toward the survival of their masters, or informing their masters of any threat against their authority.

The stature was enacted in 1710, after an attempted mutiny aboard a slave ship from Africa. In the ongoing struggle to seize the ship, a slave raise a sword to kill the captain, but a young slave stepped between the blade and the captain. The boy's arm was severed, the captain life was spared, and the assaulter was killed, crushing the mutiny. After the boy had recuperated from his injury he was rewarded for saving the captain life, and became a free man.

But that did not solve the problem of insurrection. In fact, insurrection became more adamant, and the penalties became more harsh. Flogging and hanging were frequent occurrences. There were instances of unruly slave being burned alive.

Killing slaves was a costly measure, but the slave owners had run out of options. There was nothing else they knew to do, except suffer the lost to set an example for other slaves.

In 1712, a man named Willie Lynch came to the colonies from Portugal offering a solution to the problem. His solution was a method of persuasive propaganda guaranteed (he said) to induce the slaves to give up their social alliance with each other and trust more in their taskmasters.

In substance, his method copied the method used by the Mohammedans to control the Africans back in the 6th century. Its psychogenesis were designed to alter the social genetics of the slaves through indoctrination, setting the slaves against each other: The old against the young, the woman against the man, the house slave against the field slave, the light skinned against the dark skinned, and vice versa. His method was so effective that it changed the dynamics of subjective discipline to the advantage of the white class of slave owners, and slavery eventually became an all white dominance. Slaves living under those condition turned their bitterness toward each other. What Meritorious manumission failed to achieve, the Lynch philosophy effected, causing widespread inter-racial disharmony that has continued to this day.

But the Lynch philosophy did not alter the brilliancy of those Black people. Like always, even as they questioned the loyalty of each other, many appealed to the resilient force of their imperial nature for victory, which spawned among them a variety of reactions, ranging from buying their own freedom to an odyssey of escape, each pertinent to the opportunity devised by their own ingenious strategy.

Those who bought their freedom were well versed in the intellectual pursuits of their owners, and engaged themselves in their owners' objectives to enhance the quality of their lifestyle. And when they secured their freedom they used it to further demonstrate their creative qualities, inventing gadgets and offering ideas that were beneficial to, both, the private and commercial sectors. But many weren't able to register their inventions or ideas, because of laws that barred ex-slave from obtaining or securing a patent for their products or being credited for their service to society.

Then, there were those who sought refuge in Canada after slavery was abolished in that country. Many suffered the pain of sickness and deprivation: the stinging nips of icy weather; the gruesome emptiness of hunger, and the ever-changing, never-ending hopelessness of being a homeless breed. But there was nothing so stupor to stop them, except to bury their dead. Despite the agony they faced, they continued their plight to freedom, because there was nothing they had to endure in that wilderness that was worse than the shames of oppression they had experienced as slaves.

Those who remained corralled in bondage, who had no sufficient means to escape the wrath of oppression, looked within themselves for strength to persevere. They became submerged in their religious belief to prepare them for a life in Heaven, which they thought would be better than the bitterness of slavery. Their beliefs were instilled in them by the way they understood the Bible, or the way their mastering mentors had them understand the Bible. For an example:

The King James version of the Biblical Scripture was used to interpreted the word slavery as forced servitude (bondage), which led the slaves to believe that their bondage was sanctioned by the Bible, and their submission would be rewarded in Heaver. But in reality, the word slavery stemmed from the Hebrew word, 'abad, and the Greek word diakonia, meaning to serve or to work by obligation, not by force. Nevertheless, there was forced servitude in those days, but the Bible strictly forbade it.

What the Bible did accept, though, was indentured servitude in which a man, perhaps, through poverty, who became unable to maintain himself or his family as independent citizens, could sale the rights to his labor, or the rights of a family members labor to one of his brethren that he might obtain the means of subsistence for himself and family. Even them, the obligation expired after six years of service.

Despite the many different methods the slave masters used to control their slaves many of them became free people. Some by disposition and others by disinclination, but all, even the remnants, were part of a legacy that was weaved into the fabric of history as an emblem of strength and perseverance. But the historian for the White cause edited historical documents to make the slaves appear ignorant and weak.

CHAPTER 5

The irony of a tragedy

In 1829 Andrew Jackson became the 7th president of the United States. Immediately after his inauguration he made a wholesale removal of all federal officials to make room for his own hand-picked appointees, a move that was not favored by his vice president, John Caldwell Calhoun. John Calhoun who had served as vice president under John Quincy Adams and had befriended some of Adams cabinet members, tried to persuade Jackson to retain some of his friends. Instead, Jackson selected a war general contrary to Calhoun liking which created an unfavorable relationship between Calhoun and some of Jackson's cabinet members. The stalemate resulted in a scandal initiated by Calhoun concerning the general's wife, and wives of other cabinets members. It was a rumor that suggested that some of the women were affiliated with prostitution before their marriage. The general was a close friend of Jackson, and as a retaliatory gesture, Jackson refused to accept Calhoun on his ticket for his second presidential bid. Calhoun became despondent because it damaged his political clout in Washington, and weakened his chance to proliferate his probabilistic ideals concerning slavery.

So, after his term under President Jackson was over, he return to South Carolina and started the nullification movement that led to the succession of Southern states from the union.

He argued that the nation was a confederation of sovereign states, and that if the Federal Government acted contrary to the rights of a minority of the states, this minority could secede through exercise of its sovereign rights, or could nullify Federal laws. This edited concept of sovereign laws was based, in concept, on the federal blueprint of democracy which stipulate that democracy is a form of governing in which the majority rules, but if the majority fails to take care of the minority, the minority doesn't have to follow its laws.

Andrew Jackson had induced the concept of democracy to the, then republic form of governing, to prevent the possibility of a military takeover by giving power to the people. Calhoun skillfully edited the concept to fit his traitorous scheme.

And in 1860 shortly after Abraham Lincoln was elected the 16th president of the united states, seven Southern states seceded from the union.

War was endorsable, but it wasn't Lincoln who started the war. Although, he was determined to preserve the union, it was the confederate army who fired the first shot.

The claim that the war was started to free the slaves is a lie. (Abraham Lincoln owned slaves, himself) The war was started to save the union, but it took the freedom of the slaves to win the war.

As the slaves learned of their freedom, they hastened to volunteer for duty in the union army, joining up with already free Black men to forms the few colored regiments allocated by the war general. These small forces turned the tides of the war. For, the courage and valor of those Black soldier was so adamant that it made it impossible for the confederate army to persevere. They marched through South Carolina,

Alabama, Mississippi, and Louisiana flaunting their valor as they fought their way over the hills and dales that held the graves of their ancestors: Farm land that was once wetted by their sweat and tears; Hills and Wolds that once hid their friends and neighbors from the lashes of the whip. The memories must have been mournful, but the opportunity to destroy the hate that swung those whips must have been exhilarating.

One of the earliest encounter in which Black soldiers engaged with the enemy was in 1863 at Fort Wagner on Morris Island in South Carolina. It was there that the Black soldiers of the Fifty-fourth Massachusetts regiment distinguished themselves.

William H. Carney, a sergeant with that regiment, although wounded himself, picked up the American flag when its bearer was killed and led the charge against the Confederate army. Carney was wounded twice in battle, but his determination to destroy the haters kept him on his feet.

In the spring of the year before, Robert Smalls, a Black seaman on board of the Confederate ship 'Planter' took the wheel of the Planter and sailed it out of Charleston toward the Union Navy, which was off shore. He then surrendered the ship to the Union Navy and was commissioned as the ship's pilot. He was later promoted to captain in the Union Navy. After the war, Smalls served his country as a congressman from South Carolina.

In the remaining years of the war Blacks fought many major battles but had to endure unusual hardship because of their color. They had to brave the winters with insufficient foot gear and clothes, and on many occasion their food supply and ammunition were scarce. Knowing these conditions, Confederate general Nathan B. Forrest employed tactics aimed at the annihilation of one of the units of those suffering soldiers. So many were killed that the battle was later called the Fort Pillow Massacre. But the fall of those soldiers did not tarnish the valor of their comrades. Those who survived the skirmish dusted themselves off and rose to the occasions that brought victory to the Union army.

The Civil war was one of the most tragic incidents in American history, but it paved the way for the United States to reverse its attitude toward human engineering to become the most progressive nation in the world, a progress to which the ingenuity of its Black citizens added an excellence. From 1865, through the civil right struggles in the 60s and 70s, and to this day, the brilliancy of the Black people is well in play in making this country great. But the shroud of bigotry has suppressed the valor of those Black patriots.

So, why is racial bigotry still in play here? Is it jealousy, or fear? Or is it a crutch the bigots prop themselves upon to feel superior? And when the sense of that superiority is threatened they turn to hate to defend themselves? If the latter is true, why haven't they realized that hate is an aversion derived from fear, and fear is the reaction of weakness and insecurity. Aren't they intelligent enough to realize that such psychological impairment is the stigma of a deranged mind? In dealing with that question, one may wonder if a deranged mind can be aware if its derangement.

CHAPTER 6

White, Race or Breed?

STOP and analyze yourself before you read this chapter. If you are a White Caucasian who is proud in feeling superior to others and is sensitive to the truth, this chapter may offend you.

The contents of this Chapter are the result of extensive research concerning the origin of races and skin color.

A race is class of individuals sprung from the same genetic stock of their primal ancestor. The primal, genetic stocks of the world derived from three families, Noah's sons and their wives who were the progenitors of the new generation of man. It was during their life time that the dispensation of the races were forged, and migrated to inhabit the world. Any class of people that can't be traced back, in a direct line, to those genetic stocks defined by the history of that dispensation is not a race, but a breed.

A breed is the product of a mixed-race ancestry whose off springs have not reentered his true race line. Example: When none relatives of two different races marries and bare off springs, the genetics of those two parent are mixed. Thus, the true race of that off spring cannot be biologically defined and is, therefore, called a breed. But the male gender of a certain breed can return his genetics back to the original race by marrying into his progenitor-father's race line. Usually cousins of that race line.

The first line of half breed to be confirmed by history was the linage of Ishmael. He was the by-product of a Hebrew father and an Egyptian mother, two different genetic stocks. Ishmael's mother was of the stock of Ham, but Esau, Abraham's grandson by Isaac, recovered part of Abram's genetics when he married into Ishmael's family, but there were sons of Ishmael who took for themselves Canaanites wives, and continued the linage of half breeds, which are identified among the Arabs. Nevertheless, they still claim Abraham as their ancestor.

By this, it could be said that Jesus was a breed. Not so! Although, Ruth, an ancestor-mother of Jesus was not a Hebrew, she was of the linage of Shem, the same genetic stock as Boaz. Therefore, the genetics of her off spring returned to the genetic line of the Hebrews who ascended from Shem.

Although, some of Ishmael's off springs had cohabited with the Canaanites, and produced off springs, through confusion of the Arabs genealogies their identity with the Canaanites was lost, but Biblical reference reckons them among the sons of Canaan, which makes them Canaanites, and since the Canaanites were consecrated under a curse to be servants in the house of Shem (Gen. 9: 25, 26), it is reasonable to assume that Gehazi, the servant of Elisha, was a Canaanite, Being that Elisha was of the house of Shem, and Gehazi was his servant.

The name Canaan or Canaanite is a Hebrew word signifying sunburn, brown-skinned-color with a purplish texture, which means that Gehazi was a man of color. (There is no record in history that implicates Gehazi to any other race but the Canaanites.)

Elisha, a prophet of the BC era, about 925 BC, cursed Gehazi with the stigma of leprosy and turned his skin white (2 Kings 5:27), declaring that "The leprosy therefore of Naaman," the man Elisha had just healed of leprosy, "shall cleave unto him and his seed forever". And Gehazi went out from the present of Elisha a leper as white as snow, which mean that he became genetically colorless. He was cursed with a skin condition that is congenitally deficient in pigment that became a hereditary trait of his off spring. And being that Gehazi ascended from a marriage Ishmaelites and the Canaanites, he could be considered a breed, and all of his off springs are breeds, not a race.

As the seeds (off springs) of Gehazi grew in numbers, their genetics code spread throughout the world, permeating into others races, destroying the effectiveness of their pigmentation system to imparted their inheritable genetics to all whom they had intercourse with.

Today, the term 'White people' is used figuratively to address the pale skinned people of the Caucasian or Caucasoid heritage. Nevertheless, as the result of inter-marital relationship the skin color of the Caucasian people varies, ranging from dark brown to white. The truth is that every race has white and Brown skinned people, even the Black race. But the linage of the Caucasians can be traced back to Canaanites, assuredly through Gehazi.

The Caucasian or Caucasoid people derived out of the Circassians who were indigenous to a region of mount Caucasus in Asia.

History does not account for the time of their ancestry, but it does trace them from the Merovingian Franks of the 6th and 8th back to the Canaanite heritage. The Franks were a Germanic people whose warriors overran the Roman Empire during the early Christian era, But, an extensive analysis of history found that they are not an authentic race of people, nor were they ever distinguished as a nation until the 16th century AD despite their medieval existence. Their existence is signified with the old Phoenicians who were Semitic and were known as remnants of Canaanites after their sovereignty was destroyed by the Hebrews under Joshua's leadership. The term, Caucasian did not enter into the English language to describe them until 1807 AD, and the term 'White man' or 'pale Face' was not used to describe the Caucasians until the Indian uprising during the late 19th Century AD.

The Franks (Germanic people) from which they derived was a barbaric people, lacking in culture and refinement until around the 16th Century AD. About midway through the renaissance, between the 14th and 17th century, their post leprous heredity had prevailed considerably in that region, resulting in a white-skinned majority. Thus, a change was noted in their culture, marked by a transformation in their humanistic values, and expressed in the appreciation of fine arts and classical literature, which effected a decorum of etiquette that changed the tone and texture of their lifestyle, possibly caught up in the same cultural transformation as the rest of Europe. But, however, it was from the resolution in the late 1700s AD that they emerged with an imperialistic tug of ethnic pride of themselves. And to satisfy that pride they sought distinction by introducing their subtleties in the form of customs and moral standards pertinent to their imperialistic ideology.

As years passed, those customs and standards were translated into fundamental practices, which were expressed in part by a consciousness crouched in terms of racial supremacy.

Many of the Caucasians migrated into other countries, and took with them the assumption that they were a pure race of people, guising their true heritage in a set of stratagems that launched them to prominence, mostly because the knowledge of the Ecclesiastic imprecation that had turned their skin pale (White) had vanish into the hushed voices of history, and others who were aware of the stigma chose to keep it there to benefit from the distinction their white skin had drawn to them.

By the end of World War 1, their imperialistic pride had turned into ethic bigotry, and in 1933 it began to manifest itself in a man named

Adolf Hitler. Hitler was anti-Semitic and acquired a large following from various groups of the Caucasian persuasion who were also anti-Semitic. Their Anti-Semitic sentiments were more of a heritage than a perception, stemming from their ancestor, Gehazi who resented the Jews because of the curse imposed upon him by Elisha, even though the stigma of post leprosy syndrome invaded the Jewish heritage. (Post leprosy syndrome as used here is a symptom, such as white skin, that remains in a human being after the body has completely recovered from the leprose macules. This is the symptom the Hebrew priest used to determine when a leper was completely healed).

Much confusion has arisen concerning the scriptural allusions to leprosy. The English interpretation of the disease, elephantiasis Graecorum, is totally different in its symptom, course, and termination from the Leviticus and New Testament leprosy. The English version of leprosy as we know it is a constitutional, incurable, and more or less contagious disease, which begins with numbness of the extremities, with or without pain. It causes dusky and livid swellings, and distortions of the hands and feet; ulcers upon the soles of the feet. These extend to the bones, crippling the victim. And often after a long and miserable life, the victim succumbs.

The Leviticus or Biblical leprosy is a whiteness (Exod. 4: 6) which disfigured its victim's skin, but did not disfigure him. Naaman and Garzi in the 5th chapter of 2nd Kings went about as ordinary human beings. The victims of this form of leprosy were unclean only as long as the affection was partial. Once the whole body lost the intensity of its color (Became white) it represented a terminus of the virus and the victim was declared cleaned, but the condition of a cured person is hereditary, not contagious. (2nd King 5: 27), which is the result of pale skinned (White) people.

Presumably of course, over many years of frustration with their paleness, which is evidential of their efforts to tan their skin, the effort to deal with their paleness was translated into a style of rhetorical elocution, which may have been methodical of "I'm White and I'm proud", that made them proud of their skin color, which elevated into a decorum of ethnic pride.

Pride create conceit, and conceit is embodied in a spirit that strives to protect the inordinate self-esteem of that individual.

In a fundamental sense it is an imaginative concept that represents the merging of two extremes, envy and hate. Envy is the resentful awareness of a difference enjoyed by another, while hate is an emotional attitude arising from pain, fear, or jealousy. Together they are a kind of self-generating enmity that provokes impulsive resistance in thought and principles. Such resistance can be translated into offensive behavior and qualify an opportunity for a pervert to satisfy his or her sadistic urges such as lynching rape, and sadomasochism toward those they have subjected to their chauvinistic hate.

Such a hate can stimulate sexual fanaticism in a sex pervert when the urge to satisfy it is so intense that it began to affect the neurocrine activity of the hormones. To the perpetrator it may feel like a natural trait, justified by their self-righteous attitude, but in reality it's a sadistic perversion.

Is hate a perversion, then? I say not. Hate and anger is of the same nature in the sense that they are impulses that are born out of pain and succumbs in pleasure. Their anatomy is pleasure and pain: the pain of injury and the pleasure of vengeance. Thus, the pleasure of hate and anger is the feeling that gratification will be achieved as a result of revenge. But, more often than not, that act of revenge is more offensive than defensive. And to a sex pervert, it is an exhilarating experience.

After fudging the concept that white skin represented a pure race of people, the Germans, who were called Nazi under Hitler's rule, poured out their hate on a whole race of people in an atrocious masquerade of ethic offensiveness called the holocaust.

Before then, this same manner of hate enslaved, tortured, and killed millions of Black people in the United States, both slaves and free people, even before Hitler was born. But the atrocities committed against the slaves and Blacks in the United States were in essence sacrificial rituals rather than racial extinction. The lives of the slaves and free Blacks were sacrificed for the sake of authority. The White man wanted power of authority over the Black race, and they generated an aura of hate to achieve it. For, hate is the most hostile of all impulses. It implies an emotional aversion from moral ethic so odious that it outrage the sense of what is right.

But such hate has no real power of its own: no powers to suppress, destroy, or subject anyone to its hostile nature; nor does it empower the hater to do so. It is the potency of authority, which is the ability to influence or command thought, that give power to the hater. Once an individual, or individuals, concedes to the authority of a hater, he gives up his authority to govern himself and become a victim of his hater. And the fate of the victims is determined by the inherent impulses of the hater, which with the bigoted white man is a sadistic stratagem.

CHAPTER 7

The Irony of Authority

The white man used and still uses many different stratagems to steal the Black man's authority. First he created two different social worlds. During slavery it was the world of the field slave and the world of the house slaves. After the Civil War it became the White world and the Black world. Then he proceeded to put enmity between those two worlds by establishing White neighborhood and Black neighborhood; Whites schools and Black schools, Whites churches and Black churches. Even the graves yards were separated.

This separation made it easier to legislate laws that made it legal for the hater to terrorize the Black communities with his sadistic behavior patterns, ravishing the Black neighborhoods with arson, pillage, and death, rendering them powerless to defend themselves. For, any effort the Black community made to defend themselves was treated as a threat to the White man's life, and the participants were arrested and sometimes lynched. The reality, here, was that if the White man wanted you dead, death was inescapable.

The motive for these subjective measures was plain and simple: It, figurative speaking, pushed the Black man into a corner and gave him an alternative: give up your authority or your life.

Authority is an individual asset. As adults, each individual has the power of his own authority, and the scope of an individual's authority is reckoned by the integrity of that individual. Integrity used here simply means having the power to control and command events instrumental to your own destiny. That power can be easily weaken by psychological tactics. Tactics that are predicated on fear and hopelessness. In essence, fear and hopelessness are the only means one's power can be compromised. But fear alone can't weaken a man's will; it provokes one to defend himself. But, the affects of hopelessness will turn fear into a sense of reverence toward the hater: a self-denying awe that effects submission to that which has a domineering influence over your life.

In essence, it's a psychosocial kind of strength-sucking technique that strips one of all his or her positive strengths, such as courage, self-sufficiency, self-esteem, self-willed, and, moreover, a sense of importance, leaving one to depend on anything external to his or herself. It starts with suppressive indoctrination to alienate one from his fundamental attributes and beliefs, to accept contrasting regimented ideas while using fear tactics that induces dread or despondence. And to maintain that authority, suppressive measures must ensue, even if it means a show of force. Of course, leeching of this sort is sometime used by parents, politicians, marriage couples, and religious minister to govern their constituency, but hardly to the extent of suppression of one's rights and will to exist. But a bigot whose prime objective is to suppress his victims has no limits to which he will go to achieve that authority.

When force is not convenient to use, the bigot resorts to defamation of character in an attempt to destroy the Black man's authenticity. It was widely use in Europe during the war. The White soldiers spread rumors that the Black soldiers were hoodlums and rapists and they had to use prison and ropes to keep them in check.

During the Korean War, the White soldiers claimed that the Black soldiers had tails. There were incidents in which the Koreans asked Black soldiers to show their tails. Many Black soldier in combat were shot in the back by White bigots who claimed that they were cowards. There were complaints of such behavior, but the complaints never left the front lines.

When the war ended in Korea, the Black soldiers came home to be slapped in the face by the Jim Crow practices of the South. It was a devastating blow that every Black soldier in the United Stated had to suffer. Job opportunities for them were scarce compared with demands. The few jobs that were offered to Blacks were menial with salaries commensurate to the poverty level. The pursuit of an education was a struggle. With what little chance they had, which was the GI bill of rights, they paid their way through trade schools to enhance their chances for better jobs, but the markets still denied them the compensation they deserved. To feed their families they labored on construction job under the hot summer's sun, and through intensely cold winter blizzards, and to soften their trying aches, some turned to alcohol and drugs, and others forsook their families to make them eligible for welfare.

But Black veterans living under these condition, who went to war to support the cause for the freedom of this country, still clung to the belief that they deserved the freedom and opportunities enjoyed by their White counter parts, and they strove harder for intellectual guidance to deserve a compensatory balance in the political and economical affairs of this country.

But the Whites who were in power continued to limit the amount of education and opportunities available to the Black communities, and tried strategically to disfranchise them at the ballot box by devising a panoply of rules and penalties to keep them off the ballot. But that wasn't enough to hold the Black man in check, so they took their stratagem to the badge, justifying acts of police brutality to build up a dominance they thought would condition the black communities to cope with the little they had without rebelling. But the Black communities were well aware of the abundant of resources that were available to the White communities and felt that they deserved an equal chance to access those resources. But their prospects were just a figure of their hopes.

Nevertheless, the Black man wasn't willing to further comprise his authority. Though his history had been kept from him, he felt a genius that lay dormant within his nature, an extraordinary intellectual power that had been forced into quiescence by suppression. It was like an awareness of a thinking being locked away into the deep reaches of his personality trying to surface, but he felt helpless to retrieve it.

During those years, the fate of many Black veterans could be summed up in a poem a Korean War veteran wrote in reminiscence of his once homeless experience. He named it "Sparrow in the Storm":

"I am like a sparrow in the storm,
Drifting alone over a barren desert plain;
	Contending to escape the wind's harm,
With no roost or shelter from the rain.

	I cry out for help, my eyes are my voice.
My struggle is like an open book.
	I am no beggar, but I have no choice,
But no one bother to even take a look.

	Neither is there one with a listening ear,
Nor with a hand reached out to take hold.
	I look for mercy but none is near,
Just those lonely nights and chilling cold.

My flesh turns numb by the icy winds,
My limbs shoot forth like a lifeless tree.
    I appeal to God to forgive my sins,
And asked if he would think to rescue me.

    In that hour when a dream come to mind,
When slumber finally came despite the pain,
    A glimmer of hope seemed would shine,
But was quickly douched by the pouring rain.

    I laid my case before the world's eye,
And appealed to the fair sense of man.
    Why does misery fall on one such as I?
Who helped to deliver you from the enemy's hand?

    Grief doesn't sprout up from the earth,
Nor is pain conspired by the wind.
    It's the works of men that give them birth,
Out of their thought do vices ascend.

    So, why am I burden with this curse?
What reason is there to relegate me?
    Have I not paid my way from my own purse?
And provided for my own debauchery?

    Have I said to you 'Give me this or that?'
Or taken from you anything that was yours?
    Did I not perform well when I was at bat,
And took nothing undeserving of my chores?

Why, then, am I out here where trash is thrown,
Like a sparrow in the storm, ragged and poor?
    And on a hopeless path with nothing of my own,
Except that which you pitch out your back door?

    That's nothing more than a meatless bone,
Sometime the stink of it is worst than bowel,
    Yet, I eat it for strength to struggle on.
For the same, the dogs are on the prowl.

    Who do I blame for this homeless hell?
Shall I blame God for the days that are left?
    He would be the judge and defendant as well,
And would not be divided against himself.

    Have I made an error, not knowing of my offense?
Or failed to serve the purpose for which I was made?
    Though, I think myself innocent in a virtuous sense,
Only God knows if I have a debt to be paid.

    For this country, I was willing to give my life.
To surrender my soul for the freedom of this land.
    But there's no honor for me, just pain and strife,
And to live a life below the dignity of man.

    Are you so high that you can't see your foot?
Or did you deliberately step on me?
    The tree from which you eat I saved its root,
And all you can give back is misery?

The eagle nestles away from harm.
The bear hibernate in a safe redoubt
    But I'm force to live here in the storm
With only a hope to help me out."

And it was the courage and a commitment to himself as an authenticate man that turned his hope into a reality to escape the storms of oppression which caused his homelessness. It was an awakening that made him realized that, what the white man used to oppress him, he could use to overcome that oppression. If he, as a Black man, was willing to sacrifice his life against the foes of freedom in a foreign land, he should be willing to do the same against the foes of freedom on his home turf.

He suddenly realized that his submissiveness to the White man's authority was not because he had violated any laws, but because he had become to revere the White man. The White man's subversive tactics, such as pillory and Psychological indoctrination had instilled so much fear in the Black citizens of this country that the subconscious awareness of the Black man/woman was narcotized into a sense of reverence. And it was in this sense of reverence that the black man had retained himself from rebelling against the White man authority. The same way he retain himself from rebelling against the principle of a god he believe in. It could be said that the White man was treated like a demigod.

This awakening was not just the conviction of one man, but of thousand of Black men and women throughout the United States. It brought them together in one of the most meaningful uprising since the revolutionary war-The Civil Rights Struggle.

But, there is, in afterthought, a startling realization of an error that was made in the eventualities of the civil right struggle. It is as vivid as the crimson of the evening sun; and as pronounced as a tempestuous cloud on a stormy day. It is the failure of our leaders to encourage or instill a sense of civil dignity along with the sense of civil rights. Their failure has resulted in a morality sloth that is slowly destroying the usefulness of human relationship, and when it reaches its peak the conscious of a human being will be no different than the instincts of an animal. In essence, intellectual reasoning will be over shadowed by instinctive reaction.

Of course, there will be some exceptions, and those exceptions will rise to rule over our communities.

The instinctive thinker will regard his or her imagination as a reasoning faculty and their emotions as a guide to conduct. Always, there will be something beyond their ability to understand, and they will interpret that ignorance as an awareness that what they don't understand doesn't really exist. So their response will be to follow their emotions and act in a way their emotion leads them.

Stop a moment and analyze what I've just said about the clarity of understanding. If you didn't understand what I meant, did you think that it was a nonsensical assumption of me that didn't merit your research?

If so, from that conclusion, if collective shared, the pitiful and familiar story of the harsh realities of the past will be replayed.

Many errors in our pursuit for equal opportunities and justice have been made because of a lack of understanding the principles of progress. It seemed that the bulk of our leadership have acted without intellectual prudence, understanding the results of what they do and say. Or, they have acted on their own behalf. Those who did called themselves Black leaders and enjoyed the financial rewards of it, leaving much of the Black communities to rot in the mire of their own misconception.

An explanation for this shocking perception is demonstrated every day in our neighborhood, our schools, and in our churches. It is evident in the conduct of our young generation, which is a reflection of the parenting generation: Young boys parading themselves as social bullies, focusing more on sports than rational intelligence; and young girls flaunting themselves as sex magnets. Those who are not pushing a baby carriage are focused more on cellular relationship than preparing themselves for adulthood. Their mannerism reflects a dependency on external sources, like puppets of some kind of wanton spirit.

What is the source of such a wayward character? Can we blame it all on their parents? Fathers who have deserted them, mothers who cannot appreciate the values of a strong father image in the family, or is it something else? I would say it's all of the above, especially the "something else".

That "something else" could be friends, neighbors, communities centers workers, or the entertainment media. The outward events of the family's intra-structure, without strong parental guidance, can be a hindrance as well as an asset in moral growth of a youth. It depends upon the kind of culture that "something else" carries.

Each one of us is a culture carrier. Our convictions, our attitude, our temperament, and the choices we make are reflections of the culture that is partial to our philosophical makeup. And it is contagious. What happens around our children affects their perception, and can become a culture builder.

Our children are perceptive like we are. What they hear, sees, feels or smells become a part of their perception as information to be recycled through their thinking process. The way they process that information defines their ability to understand what they perceive. The ability to understand comes through insight. They understand by identifying certain items that can be combined into image that seem meaningful to them. And if they are confronted with an item that they cannot identify with something else, or if they identify that item with something contrary to its real nature, chances are that individual's experience will be contrary to truth, and without intellectual guidance, that individual will become a part of a culture indicative of the way he or she experienced that item.

To make choices that are potentially meaningful to them, they will select items from a vortex of data that they get from perceptual guideline. Therefore, parent should be discreet in deciding what their children are exposed too, because out of their own experiences evolves a personal vision of the world. And it is this vision that becomes the designer of their behavior. If this vision is conceived out of imaginative data their whole life will be structured on empty presumptions.

The danger in that is that presumptuous outlooks on life always overlook the meaningful factors that connect the events that continue a successful process. If one item in the chain of event that produce successful results is omitted or compromised by lack of actuality, the chain collapse and the trend is interrupted.

Such behavior patterns created thousand of slum houses in the Black communities, families with no fathers, and mothers who cannot cope with the difficulties of managing a single parent family.

As this difficulty work upon the experiences of the families, the neighborhood in which they live become a stigma of that difficulty, and that stigma is the diagnostic sign of a behavior pattern that is inconsistent with acceptable standards, manifested in waves of crime, silly fads and unconventional changes in social taste. These patterns develops in such a gradual and imperceptible degree that they become fixed into the environment before any real affects are noticed. By then, the mode and manner of those patterns have begun to attract instrumentalities that further affect the tranquility of that community, isolating that community into a culture of violence and hysteria.

And as those young people grow up, they began to look at society with a painful an unwarrantable sense of exclusion, not understanding why they have to live on a social plane where the world looks at them with prejudice. Their lives are a continuous challenge to themselves and others. Right or wrong, their behavior is like a swinging pendulum, swaying from despair to elation, each movement carries with it an attitude that defeats their chances to develop their real potentials. They exist as contingents, not as primacies, having their intelligence darkened by phantasm, and in my opinion, subject them to the most abject form of living condition known to man, which is servility.

Servility is the spiritless awareness of oneself as a dependent being, leeching on others, solely to imitate a lifestyle that is out of their reach, resulting in a perception of imagery and ideals that defies common sense. The contingents of such a life style have no real goals, no productive perspectives, except to leech and gratify themselves on flattery and meaningless guises. The danger in this is that such a perception grew up with them, and it became the legacy of their children.

It is hard for me to imagine how our Black leaders can allow such condition to persist, and yet expect to achieve an equitable relationship with successful neighbors.

In my opinion, if our Black leaders exert more efforts directly toward upgrading the character of our youth rather than their 401K these conditions could not survive.

I do believe that the Black leaders of today is an insult to the Black leaders in the BC era in a sense that they have no creative guidelines to follow; no integrity from which they can draw the kind of strength and courage it takes to resurrect the superior intelligence of the Black people.

Of course, there are intellectuals among us, both White and Black, and the modernization of the world reflects that intelligence. But I am talking about the kind of intelligence that can guide us without a compass; intelligence that can teach us without books, and sustain us without compromising our safety; intelligence that is creative, not just inventive, and intelligence that deals in common sense rather than emotions. Sounds fantastic? Well, that's the kind of intelligence that started the whole human process. Every intellectual aspect of today is rooted in that primal intelligence. Such is the kind of intelligence we need in our Black leaders of today.

Since the death of Dr. Martin Luther King the quality of Black leadership has warned. Instead of positioning themselves in the forefront of the action needed to continue our progress, they are staying behind trying to push. A leader who pushes from the rear have no bearing on where we are going, even if it's back where we started from.

Our Black citizens deserves better. For more than three hundred years we have sacrificed our blood and tears to help build the most prosperous nation on earth, and we have yet to realize the full benefits of those sacrifices.

It seems that as we near the leveling point an obstacle appears and compromises that progress.

Those obstacles, usually appears in the form of obstructionism—a deliberate interference with progress in order to defame our existence as a people. But how and why is this obstructionism levered against us in the first place.

In the main, it's all about nobility. The White man strives on nobility. Without it he is lost in a perpetual sense of unworthiness with nothing to compensate for it but speculation, which is to expunge the haunting image of his incommensurable past. His sense of mobility shields him from the shame of the curse his ancestors had to suffer before the Franks conquered Rome in the fourth century AD.

It was this sense of nobility, which developed out of the behavioristic pattern of the Justinian code of law developed from the Roman law of the 6th century and expressed in the social culture of Louisiana during the slave era. By then it had become a systematic way of thinking, which contributed to their moral growth and prosperity. From it they became objective in authority and resources.

How does this affect the Black man? The answer is simple: After slavery, there were only two recognized classes of people in the United States, the White and the Negro. And in order for the White man to maintain his nobility he had to exalt himself above the Negro. Consequently, he had to continue suppressing the Negro. But seeing how brilliant the Negro was he realized that his 'Willie Lynch' philosophy could no longer give him that edge under the new federal guidelines. Therefore, he had to devise statutory amendments to the existing statures to compromise federal control of the South. Those amendments are called Jim Crow Laws.

Beginning in the late 1880s these amendments began to censor political candidates and voters, and by the turn of the century Negros had lost virtually the entire political clot they had in Washington since the Civil War.

And in 1915 the rebellious attitude of the white south began to express itself in pillage and death to resurrect and maintain their sense of nobility through a secret organization called the Ku Klux Klan. Their ideas were based on the Kultarr culture, a social organization under the Nazi persuasion that was systematic in their application of chauvinism, militarism, and terrorism.

It struck the south with such a satanic blow that the whole nation trembled: Onslaught of pillage and death plagued the South. Lynching was common place. Farms and homes were swept from sight in raging fires and smoke.

Something was happening in this country that was beyond the ethics of war. Women were raped, men were taken from their homes beaten and murdered in full view of their neighbors. Property was confiscated as spoils leaving families homeless with no shelter from inclement weather, but if they rebelled the law would take over and finish the works of, what I would call, the posses from Hell. All this was for the sake of the White man's sense of nobility. There could be no other reason for a defenseless class of people to be subjected to such atrocious oppression.

There is a sign in the mode of things that these atrocities will soon reoccur. And, if the Black man doesn't stand up against the circumstances that are destroying the authenticity of our dignity we will fail and resort back to the servility of the 1800s. It will be a submission rather than oppression.

Every human element in the world need strong and courageous leaders: Any who allow degrading circumstances to eat away at the moral fibers of their environment are no better than the bigots who use those circumstances against us. "If you allow it, you are a part of it" is my reasoning here.

Therefore, we simply cannot rebuke the bigots for their racial improprieties without rebuking the instrumentalities that give them their pitch. We must get the trash out of our own yard before we can demand our neighbors to clean up their yard.

More than anything else, I am disappointed in those Black leaders who have enjoyed the financial fruits of the civil rights struggle to bed themselves with the white bigots. That, too, is improper, and traitorous.

I don't mean to suggest that our Black leaders should become an enemy of the state, that would be disastrous, but I do mean they should not compromise their commitment to their constituents for the sake of politics. How can they represent us when they are eating from the same dish as the bigots? And how can they rebuke the dish they are eating from without being a hypocrite?

CHAPTER 8

A Remade Man

I spent four of my ten years in California working in the midst of Hollywood's celebrities, movie stars and recording artists, Black and White. I have to admit that the experience was more disappointing than remarkable. Contrary to the drama they portray on screen and on stage, their real life experiences were as ordinary as ghetto brats. And the airs of their behavior, which are reflected in their drama, are conducive to a ghetto brat mentality. The only different in their style of conduct was how they reacted to the elegance of their surroundings. If the elegance wasn't there, they would give the impression that they were bred among the uncivilized.

Of course, that doesn't spoil their success, but it does define their character, in which they take comfort in being what they are. And being what they are conveys a subliminal message to their admirers, our youth, which have a formative effect on their character. In essence, our youth become impressed by the manner of their expressions and feel impulsive to mimic that expression.

Take notice! The disposition of today's entertainers is hardly commendable, but it gives them fame and fortune. And it is this fame and fortune that attracts the interests of our youth. And the psychological effects it has on the formative minds of those youth will create within them an envy instrumental of those effects and the excitement they feel determines how they deal with their experiences. They will stitch those effects with what they think is important to them and develop a character they think will make them acceptable to those who are likewise entertained by those celebrities. Its like, "birds that likes fish shares the same dish".

It is an ever-changing, never-ending scenario that builds a world of fantasy for our youth that will drive their mentality for years. Some will overcome and some will not. Those who will not overcome will go about life in a maze of confusion, dealing in stimulants and accessories to help them deal with the real world that they had rejected during their youth. Those stimulants could be drugs, alcohol, or perverted adventures; those accessories could be friend, clothes and other material things that give them a sense of importance. In either case, they become lost in an ideology that had no moral meaning to them. To them, God exist only in the imagination of those who object to their life style. It is a highly geared lifestyle full of conflict and confusion, a lifestyle that is based on perverted sensations, imperiously drives them to satisfy their sensual urges at the expense of shortening their life span, and perverting the morals of their communities. It is a lifestyle in which sensual pleasure is an addiction. Like alcohol, they take stiff drinks of it and become exulted in its inebriety. When that exultation wears off the emotions dries up leaving them in a listless void that haunts them like a dead spirit. To overcome this hunting dullness, they wonder deeper into the perverted world of pleasure, and soon become pleasure-holics, surrendering daily to the compulsive force of their obsession.

Nothing else matters to them but their pleasure. Their children, too, are left without intellectual guidelines, growing up in an environment characteristic of and appropriate to wildness, dispossessed and disinherited.

Youth is the time of life marked by growth and development, usually between childhood and majority. An individual learns more between that age than they do for the rest of their life. They learn by identifying themselves with the complexities of their experiences. There is nothing else they can learn from except their experiences. And there is nothing else that textures their character the way their experiences do. Therefore, anyone who is instrumental in determining the nature of those experiences should be remembered.

There is no doubt that our youth are subordinate to the drama and glitter of the entertainment industry, and that the celebrities of that industry supplies the experiences of that glitter and drama that personify the imagination of our youth, and steer them to regard their imagination as a guideline to how they express themselves to the world. So, they adapt the attitude and behavior they feel comes with that expression, and they use it as a definition of power. And because of their lack of informed judgment they are unable to realize the affects their expression will have on others. As a result they are confronted with an array of reactions that confuses their imagination and they are left with a challenge that may seem threatening to their objectives. To confront it, they become arrogant and defiance as a show of strength. But what they really show is an attitude that defies any kind of correction. So they are left alone to struggle with their frustration. And that frustration turns into animosity tending toward something they don't really understand. It's like some unknown foe is challenging their existence, and because they don't recognize what it is, they see it in everybody they confront, not knowing that it's their ignorance that is their foe. All because they defied intellectual guideline for experiences in drama and glitter. They are too unknowing to realize that what they think they know is not all to be known.

The celebrities who supply these experiences cares little about the mess our communities are in so long as they are being enriched by the dollars our youth spend on their behalf.

Despite the fear, the violent, the sense of exclusion, and emotional aches that they have caused our communities to suffer, they still cling to the idea that their behavior is a constitutional right—and they are right. Every individual in the United States have the right to behave as they choose, but it's not their rights that are at stake here, it's their behavior. And there are laws that censor behavior when it is contrary to acceptable standards. When individuals have conducted themselves in a fashion that threaten our lives or trends to destroy our moral standards, the law holds them liable. Therefore, the laws that are already in existence can be used to hold these celebrities liable for the damage their influence had caused our communities to suffer, such as accessory to inciting public violent, or tumult when that incitement represent a tort. It would give parents and victim of crimes that are influenced by the behavior of celebrities a tool to fight the onslaught of depravity that is consuming our communities. If the influence of celebrities is translated into damages, make them compensate for that damage. And if the question of constitutional rights come into play, remember that there is nothing right about immorality, especially the kind that is destroying the civility of our communities.

In my opinion, the high school massacre in Colorado a few years back is an example of how influential and dangerous screen drama can be. There were indications that the shooting was inspired by a movie drama that led to a domino-like affect of school shooting across the country. Had it not been for that move, the imagination of that first perpetrator may not have taken on such an hostile form against his peers. Of course, that is just an opinion, but the symptoms of his behavior reflected a resemblance to the experiences of the movie. And it was reveal that he had seen that movie, and had dress like one of its characters. I dare not mention the name of the movie for fear that it may resurrect interest in that movie.

I have notice, too, that most all of the movies I have seen, of all sort, have been chauvinistic toward the white male personage. His image as leading character has always been portrayed as the hero: The conqueror or the savior. Even in movie with black leading characters, the white male image has defined the success of the story, which in effect, gives him a false sense of superiority

Well, I don't read too much harm into that, except that it has characterized him as a redeemer, which carries with it an exaggerated opinion of him that cannot pass the reality test. And it is suggestive of an effort to exploit the imagination of the people to vision the White man as having superlative courage and authority in the face of all odds. In some cased the vision warped the mentality and gives one an exulted sense of dominance that makes him or her feel that they are the judge and executioner.

It is true that there are white individuals who deserve such praiseworthy and honorable definition, so do many individuals in all other races, but it should not become a vision of authority.

The movies are trying to isolate the definition of a hero to the White male image to maintain his noble standings in society, but to suggest it as a racial trait is preposterous. The White man deserve being considered as a noble being if you regard exploitation, extortion, and pillage as credits for a noble standing.

Of course, we cannot blame the White man for his behavior, but we can blame ourselves, because we endorsed it. We endorsed it with submissive grandiloquence and gestures, and performed extraordinary tasks for menial compensation. We suffered poverty to raise him to riches, and we compromised our dignity to condone his insults.

It's time for a revival: A renewed attention to our brilliancy; a renewed presentation of our courage and perseverance, but most of all a revitalization of our noble spirit.

We must cast off that ex-slave mentality, chip away that ignorance of a man, and carve out a new image of ourselves. And stand before the world and say, "Here I am, a remade man".

Here forth are odds of my revival:

Once I looked upon life through foolery,
    Arrogant and unlearned I drifted to and fro.
    Misunderstanding and cynicism were my mode daily,
    And I was destined only to poverty and strife.

Though, I sought to escape life's barren places,
    My efforts were futile and confounded.
    Hopelessness swiftly overtook me,
    And I became trapped in the pit of naught.

I idled daily in an air of ignorance,
    And came upon others who were likewise unlearned.
    They followed after me, pursuing my course.
    Then they went ahead of me intriguing me further.

Like madmen they corrupted whoever they befriended.
    A displeasure stemmed up and overwhelmed me,
    And I became sadden by their debased acts,
    For such as they performed bothered me.

Seeing they were without heart and mercy
    I reframed from them and fled.
    I sought refuge in such places they were not;
    From their isles I escaped and tarried far off.

I made my dwelling place a secret to them,
    Lest they discover me and assail me,
    For I had rejected them and their deeds,
    And they hated me because I reframed from them.

My resort was a strange place before me.
    I understood not the ways of its populace.
    Their mannerism was not of my awareness,
    And their deeds were fashioned after intelligence.

I marveled exceedingly, seeing them of such behavior,
    Yet I understood not the manner of their mode.
    Yes, but an impulse of delight came over me;
    So intriguingly, the impulse of envy overwhelmed me.

Surely, I had cause to be inquisitive of this novelty,
    And I confronted an old man alone in his saunter.
    I implored him to interpret the ways of this place,
    And he stopped awhile and paid me some attention.

In his gentlemanliness he divulged his knowledge.
    My perception became clear and I envisioned it.
    Truth, in its real image, led me henceforth,
    And I walked in its light and I was no longer confused.

There stood before me both wisdom and knowledge,
    Forthright, I reach out and milked them,
    Because their breasts were filled with reality,
    And I had need for the genuineness therein.

I became crowned by a great faith in God;
    My crown was living wisdom within me.
    I became matured in the knowledge of his word,
    And I was loosed from all vanity and foolishness.

Daily, I lifted up my voice to the most high,
    And I praise him for his name sake.
    I beseeched his mercy and his guide successfully,
    No more did I fall away from his strength.

No longer do I suffer the dregs of ignorance,
    Nor do I regard the teaching of fools.
    For they know nothing beyond their own foolishness,
    Nor do they teach anything that is wise.

There are two things in life that entices me,
    One thing I seek from their works:
    Wisdom and knowledge, they comfort me;
    With them I will reach for greatness.

Wisdom is like a king that oversees his Kingdom.
    Knowledge is like a prince that interprets his law.
    Together they build a fortress from disaster,
    And a shelter from the violent of ignorant storms.

Where ignorance dwell many are made inferior,
 And they go about laboring for inferior things.
 Fear overwhelm them and submission sets in,
 And they seek after something to submit too.

Wisdom light the way from the pit of naught;
 Knowledge is the ladder upon which one ascends.
 Therefore, inferiority is overcome by greatness,
 And courage invades fear and conquers it.

Verily, knowledge is the destroyer of ignorance,
 And wisdom instills knowledge with power.
 Wisdom sees all things, visible and invisible,
 And it verifies that which is worthy to learn.

Wisdom's countenance is bright and powerful.
 It spotlights those who love it, they are readily seen.
 It hammers out foolishness with pure knowledge,
 And select those endeavors that generate success.

Wisdom will not act without certainty,
 Nor will it endure without honor and dignity.
 Validity is the force of its character,
 But most profound, though, is its truths.

Where wisdom is there is no feast for the trifler,
 The folly of a fool gets no attention,
 The path of the deceitful is cut off,
 And the criminal finds no honor in his style.

Knowledge sends the liar's tongue to its death
    The villain's deed turns and assaults him.
    The wicked is destroyed by his own wickedness,
    And the godlessness of the godless will devour him.

Open up your eyes to wisdom in its pure beauty,
    And you will see greatness standing in your reach.
    The voice of knowledge will give you instruction,
    And you will climb life's stairway to success.

I am protected against the acts of the oppressor.
    Their efforts to subdue me are made void.
    Forcedly, their hands reach out to bind me,
    But wisdom tears lose their hold.

I have given of all I have achieve in life,
    And of myself I have given most.
    Yet, I have sought no receipt,
    For what I gave was truly given.

I have assailed only the onslaught of ignorance,
    Against its deeds I took my stand;
    And I fought not just for myself,
    But for those who fell against its attacks.

Now, the hairs of my head are turning grey,
    My body is surrendering to decay,
    But I feel no regrets for the deed I performed,
    For now they come back to comfort me.

Take my advice, your sons and daughters
    And your days on earth will be easily lived.
    Take nothing from life you cannot give,
    And life will give you nothing you cannot take.

                    So be it.

THE MERGING OF TWO RACES
(Black and Hebrew)

The linage of Cush, Ham's eldest son (Gen. 10:8)	The linage of Keturah, Abraham's Concibine; (First Chronicles 1:32)
CUSH	KETURAH

Seba, Havilah, Sabha, Raamah; Sablecha, Nimrod	Zimran; Joksham; Medan; Midian
Seba, Dedan	Sheba, Dedan

The families of Raamah and Joksham came together in the early colonists of, what is now known as southern Arabia, and the Kingdom which they found was, for many centuries was called the Kingdom of Sheba or Seba.

The Queen of the South mentioned in the Book of Matthew is the Queen of Sheba mentioned in 1st Kings, 10:1. She was queen of a tribe ascending from the off spring of Raamah of the linage of Cush, and Joksham of the linage of Keturah, the Ethiopian concubine of Abraham.

Moses' wife Zipporah, the daughter of Jethro was of the linage of Midian. She was an Ethiopian.

Zipporah and the Queen of Sheba is the source of million of Black Hebrews through out the world. The hatred toward the Black Race and the Jews by other nations may very well explain that.

POSTSCRIPT

An Analogue in Drama

NARRATIVE:

The thread of black mastery ran through the history of race relations in America from the very beginning of slavery. It manifested itself in every state, and was instrumental in the success of every town, city, rural, and farm district throughout these United States; even in the wild West during the Indian uprising and the outlaw days, black men as soldiers and lawmen prevailed in strength and notoriety.

There is no part of North America that the Black man didn't touch with his creative and enduring mastery.

Time after time a particular Black man soared to the heights, unchallengeable in intellect, physique, and creative perception, to manifest the genius in him. Against inextricable atrocity he remained firm in his tendency to invest his knowledge in the potentials of well being, knowing that it was not for his benefit, nor would he be credited for its usefulness.

The motive for this disenfranchisement was simple and far-reaching. The Civil War had given the Black man a share of the most prosperous land in the world (Of course, he was the root if it); and he had out numbered the Whites in many areas. Thus, the nobility of the White man was threatened, and a fierce and bitter struggle took place to discredit the Black man— to reduce his humanity to a level commensurate to social abjection, for if he had continued to manifest his mastery, he would have automatically controlled the richest land in North America; and, the social, political, and economic destiny of this country would have been in his hands.

And, perhaps, this country would not have suffered the lost of the lives of our young men and women in the wars and conflicts of the 20th century. For, the world would have respected the military might of this country as it did Africa during the days of Alexandra The Great. During that time, no nation on earth was able to defeat the military force of Africa.

The strength and success of the United States can not be estimated without including the contributory genius of the Black people.

In the spirit of History, if the incorporeal rational beings of those Back geniuses was able to become visible at will, they would rise and testify of their contributions, it would be a drama in which the archives of history would opens up and exclaim the true accomplishments of the American Blacks; and expose the conspiracy that has shrouded their intelligence for more that 200 years. Here would be the testimony of some of those heroes:

DIALOGUE:

ESTEVANCIO

"I am the spirit of Estevancio. I was taken from Africa by Prince Henry, the Navigator when I was a teenager. After seven years of indenture servitude in Spain, I became a free man and became an explorer with the

Spanish conquistador of Mexico. In 1539 I led an exploration North into the Pacific Hemisphere of America in search of the seven cities of gold. After many weeks of travel we came upon an Indian domain called Cibola. And when I learned that it was in the county of the seven cities of gold, I sent a messenger back to Mexico with news of my discovery. But while I waited for the Conquistador to arrive, I was stabbed to death by one of the renegade Indian. Because of its discovery by explorers from Mexico, it was named the New Mexico.

PAUL CUFFEE

I am the spirit of Paul Cuffee. I was born in New England in 1759, and establish a fleet of cargo vessels that shipped goods throughout the Eastern world. While traveling to different countries, I became convinced that colonization of the Sierra Leone in Africa was the answer to the plight of Negroes in the United States. In the early 1800's century I made two voyages to Africa with my own fleet and men to establish an American Negro community, but death overtook me in 1817 before I could finish my mission.

RICHARD ALLEN

I am the spirit of Richard Allen, My associate, Abaslon Jones and I established the free African society to improve the economic and social conditions of Negroes in the United States. The free Negroes of this country were being excluded from the free enterprise system by systematic, purposeful activity by White business men who took their remarkable talent as a threat. We brought the Negro communities together and created a trading empire that led the United States to being the trading capital of the world.

In 1794, Jones and I were worshiping at the St. George's Methodist Church in Philadelphia one Sunday when we were forcible removed from the church for refusing to sat in the Colored section. Jones left the Methodist denomination and became the first Negro protestant pastor in the nation. Realizing that worship could not be confined to benches reserved for Black or whites, I went on and organized the African Methodist Episcopal Church and became its first bishop.

LEMUEL HAYNES

I am the spirit of Lemuel Haynes, I was born in the year 1753 and died in 1828. With my White wife at my side, I became the first Black minister to an all white congregation in the state of Connecticut. Following the revolutionary War, I served as pastor of the Church of Torrington. During the war I had served as a minuteman under General George Washington, during which I was engaged in action in the battle of Lexington.

JOHN B. RUSSWURM

I am the spirit of John B. Russwurm. I was the owner and operator of the Freedom's Journal, an all Black news paper founded by Samuel Cornish and I in 1827. I graduated from Bowdoin College in 1826, the first Back to graduate from a college here in the United Stated. I later abandoned Journalism to become a unionist. I was involved in the power of authority to bring municipal districts into conformity with the rules and standards of the Union when they joined with other states of the Union of the United States.

MARTIN R. DELANY

I am the spirit of Martine R. Delany. I attended Harvard Medical School, but I didn't graduate. Nevertheless, I became a successful physician with a lucrative practice. I was also an editor of a weekly news paper, and later in 1852, published a chronicle of the Black people in America titled 'The Condition, Elevation, Emigration and destiny of the Colored People Of The United States. During the Civil War, I was given the rank of major, the highest-ranking Black field officer at that time. I was also a Unionist.

NARRATIVE:

During the course of reorganization and reestablishment of the seceded states in the Union after the Civil War, and after the repeal of the Black Laws of the South, many Black men began to sit in legislative branches of government throughout the Unionized states. Such recourse provided opportunities for Blacks through the Unites Stated to be recognized for their intellectual endowment.

DIALOGUE:
ROBERT BROWN ELLIOTT

I am the spirit of Robert Brown Elliott. I was one of the first Black men to serve in the government of South Carolina after the repeal of the Black Laws, serving South Carolina as both a state legislator and a United State congressman

HIRAM R. REVELS

I am the spirit of Hiram R. Revels. I was the first Black to serve in the U.S. Senate. I was appointed to the senate by the Mississippi legislature to fill the vacancy left by Jefferson David.

JOSEPH H. RAINEY

I am the spirit of Joseph H. Rainey from South Carolina. I was a self-educated Black man, and a barber by trade. Instead of being forced to serve as a laborer in the Confederate Army, I escaped and took refuge in the West Indies. After the Civil War I served my state in several offices, and was elected to four terms in the United State Senate.

SOJOURNER TRUTH

I am the spirit of Sojourner Truth. During the Civil War I served as a nurse and also a Union spy. In 1864 I met with President Lincoln as an advocate of land ownership for freedmen. As a compensatory gesture, 40 acres of land and a mule was given to families of ex-slaves.

ROBERT SMALLS

I am the spirit of Robert Smalls. I was a seaman on board of the confederate war ship, The Planter. In 1862 I took the wheels of the Planter, and three of my Black crew members and I sailed it out of Charleston toward a fleet of ships of the Union navy. I then surrendered the Planter to one of its Captains. For this I was accepted into the Union navy, compensated for my deed, and was later promoted to Captain.

After the war I served in the United States government as a congressman from South Carolina.

PINCKNEY BENTON STEWART PINCHBCK

I am the spirit of P. B. S. Pinchback. I was the first knows Black Reconstructionist to serve as governor of a Southern state. In 1872, when the governor of Louisiana was forced to resign, I was appointed acting governor for twenty-three days. In 1873, I was elected to the United States Senate but was never allowed to take my seat.

JAMES P. RAPIER

I am the spirit of James P. Rapier I served in the Alabama State's constitutional convention in 1867; and in 1872 I was elected to the United Stats Congress, where I served one term.

HENRY O. FLIPPER

I am the spirit of Henry O. Flipper. I was the first black man to graduate from the West Point Military Academy. Immediately after my graduation, I was assigned to the Cavalry as second lieutenant, where I encountered hostility from my White colleagues. My career in the military was ended by questionable circumstances in 1881. I was relieved of my commission for conduct unbecoming to an officer. Although, I was later exonerated of the conviction, I never returned to the army.

JOHN H. ALEXANDER

I am the spirit of John H. Alexander. I was the second Black man to graduate from West Point. After my graduation, I served as a Cavalry commander in the American West. My Black soldiers and I policed the open plains in order to ensure peace between the Indians and the newly arriving settlers. After my death, the army named a camp in Virginia for me.

CHARLES YOUNG

I am the spirit of Charles Young. I was the third Black man to graduate from West Point Military Academy. After many military-related achievements, I was promoted to the rank of Colonel, the highest-ranking Black soldier in the armed forces at that time. I served in Cuba during the Spanish-American War. I also served in the American West. I was sent to Liberia as military envoy. I died in Nigeria of a tropical illness.

W. E. B. DU BOIS

I am the spirit of W. E. B. Du Bois. In 1895, I was the first to received a Ph.D from Harvard in the field of history. Though, I appreciated the efforts and achievement of Booker T. Washington, I opposed his separatist philosophy by advocating social and political equality for Blacks. In 1905 I called a conference for prominent Black leaders in Niagara Falls for the purpose of organizing a Black pressure group. The conference was called the Niagara Movement. Although, it didn't grow in strength or membership during its four-year existence, it became the launching pad for the National Association for the Advancement of Colored People, of which I became editor of its official publication, The

Crisis, in 1910. By it, I was regarded as one of the major spokesmen for Black people through much of the twentieth century.

ROBERTS H. TERRELL

I am the spirit of Robert H. Terrell. I, as a prominent Washington attorney, was named a judge of the municipal bench in the District of Columbia by president Taft. My wife, Mary Church Terrell, was the most militant of women. Her career spanned over nearly four decades. She was active as a news paper writer, and as a women rights worker until she died in 1954.

NARRATIVE:

Literature was the medium through which may talented Blacks expressed themselves during and after slavery, but it wasn't until after World War 1 that their interest in theatrical arts began to awaken the dramatics of their talent. The roots of this awakening lay in part in the growing awareness among theater-goers that Black entertainers had a unique style of performing that peppered their taste for eccentric drama.

But, however, independence Black actors found it almost impossible to establish a career in the theater. Time after time, they rose in fame but before fortune they fell along the wayside, because the white theater owners and producers had limited the extent to which a Black entertainer could succeed.

Richard B. Harrison, a famous Shakespearean actor, born in 1864, had to subsidize his living by giving programs of readings—His tenor voice was entertaining, but a leading role in any dramatic performance was out of his reach. Eventually, though, he found real fame when he played the role of 'De Lard' in 'The Green Pastures' in 1930. He died five years after that performance.

Two of the distinguished black-American composers of the early twentieth century were Harry T. Burleigh (1866-1949) and Will Marion Cook (1865-1944). Burleigh wrote many songs of theatrical value. A singer of note, he performed as a soloist in many of New York churches and synagogues such as the Temple Emanu-El and St. George's Episcopal Church. Cook, who had studied music with him wrote musical dramas, musical comedies and operettas, among his works are Clorindy and St. Louis Woman.

Theatrics were not the only intrinsic aptitude of those gifted Blacks. Many were literate in poetry and creative writing.

The aesthetic perceptions of those literary authors were reflected in their works, offering enlightening epigrams to awaken the consciousness of man to the beauty of venerating thought.

Unlike the lyrics of songs assisted by musical notes, poetry needs no accessories, it alone reaches into the heart with its amusing epigrams to awaken the mind to a deeper meaning of truth.

Poetry was once used to pay tribute to the gods, both, the idol gods of the Gentiles and the God of Heaven and Earth. It is a kind of adornment of man's thoughts that add beauty to his expression.

The Holy Bible is saturated with poetry. The book of Proverbs includes short poetic aphorisms introduced as proverbs of Solomon. The book of Job is the poetic expression of the raw faith and wisdom of a man whose reverence of God was so great that pain and ostracism couldn't shake his faith.

Nevertheless, I am partial to the book of Isaiah where I find a poetic depiction of the consciousness of a man expressed in terms of the beauty of his faith in God. It was something personal and common by its very nature, venting a strong inner compulsion to reveal the awakening of the spirit in him.

The experience of that awakening is revealed in the poems and poetry of those early Black American poets such as Claude McKay's protest poem, "If We Must Die" written in response to the race riot of 1919; and Countee Cullen's "Copper Sun", written in 1927.

Then there were fiction writers of that period, among them were Rudolph Fisher, Jessie Fauset, and Eric Walrond.

Another outstanding writer who succeeded them in the 30s and 40s was Richard Wright, author of "uncle Tom's Children" and "Native Son".

Now, with regards to my objective to explore the consciousness of my readers to awaken in them a deeper sense of awareness of their potential power, I offer this epigram:

Find yourself a place in the library of knowledge;
Open up its books and read.
Roam through the pages of life and history,
To the voice of their offerings take heed'

Learn about the laws that governs your works,
And regards the arts as creative tools.
Let the spirit of God merge with your endeavors,
And study the Bible and abide by its rules.

Use the power of prudence as a laboring maul,
And hammer away at your dignity.
Select the chisels of penance and worthy straits,
Now carve out the man you wish to be.

Chip off that countenance of an emancipated slave,
Let the new statue of yourself be seen.
Discipline yourself in the ways of wisdom,
And walk with love and self-esteem.

Drink from the fountain of knowledge daily;
Let it waters wash away that selfish mess.
Take heed it waters flow not wastefully.
And you will reap the fruits of success.

God created you when his purpose first unfolded;
From the beginning your were made for fame.
But the whipcord of slavery swung its lick
And from the haters heart, your failure came.

But the spring of freedom is gushing again.
Drank of its freshness and take your stand.
With faith and truth ascend to the heights,
And say to the world, 'Here I am, the remade man.

The mastery of the Black people of today account for itself, but it is made public and promoted only when it is to the advantage of the White man.

Nevertheless, we simply can't hold that as an offense against the White man. But it does signify a deficiency in our support of each other. Our resources, however meaningful they are, are never used in a direct effort to promote and enhance the quality of our own race. It seem that our tangible holdings are mostly used for sensual requirement which never equate to personal improvement. Instead, it confuses our sense of purpose and leaves us, as a hold, inefficient to manage our own survival.

Of course, this doesn't apply to every Black man or Woman, but it does apply to enough of the black people to effect a stagnation in our efforts to become an inter-sufficient people.

Instead of using our resources to promote instrumentalities that are destroying the moral fiber of our Communities, such as today's entertainment medium, we should focus more on Black enterprising, supporting Black businesses, manufacturing, and institutions that are instrumental to our success.

I have not seen a Black oriented movie or public performance since the move "Malcolm X" that didn't portray some kind of conflict in the relationship between the black man and the black woman, nor have I heard any music offered for the entertainment of our young boys and girls that is intellectually inspiring. And, yet, we are blaming violence and poverty in our communities on something other than ourselves; and depending on the government to solve our problems.

It doesn't take the government to teach our children personal respect and self-sufficiency, it take examples and encouragement. It doesn't take riches to make our neighborhood safe and socially acceptable, it takes a commitment to the principles of moral decency. It doesn't take welfare to feed our children, it takes self-sufficient parenting.

Only when a parent has exhausted every means of self-sufficiency at hand is it necessary to turn to the government. Accessories and sensual pleasures should never precede the care and concern for our children, nor should it precede their education. They are the parents of tomorrow and the caretakers of the aged. The things we build for them today, they will add to them for their children tomorrow.